Cornelia Haas · Ulrich Renz

My Most Beautiful Dream

Mon plus beau rêve

Bilingual children's picture book

with online audio and video

Translation:

Sefâ Jesse Konuk Agnew (English)

Martin Andler (French)

Audiobook and video:

www.sefa-bilingual.com/bonus

Password for free access:

English: **BDEN1423**

French: **BDFR1527**

Lulu can't fall asleep. Everyone else is dreaming already – the shark, the elephant, the little mouse, the dragon, the kangaroo, the knight, the monkey, the pilot. And the lion cub. Even the bear has trouble keeping his eyes open ...

Hey bear, will you take me along into your dream?

Lulu n'arrive pas à s'endormir. Tous les autres rêvent déjà – le requin, l'éléphant, la petite souris, le dragon, le kangourou, le chevalier, le singe, le pilote. Et le bébé lion. Même Nounours a du mal à garder ses yeux ouverts.

Eh Nounours, tu m'emmènes dans ton rêve ?

And with that, Lulu finds herself in bear dreamland. The bear catches fish in Lake Tagayumi. And Lulu wonders, who could be living up there in the trees?

When the dream is over, Lulu wants to go on another adventure. Come along, let's visit the shark! What could he be dreaming?

Tout de suite, voilà Lulu dans le pays des rêves des ours. Nounours attrape des poissons dans le lac Tagayumi. Et Lulu se demande qui peut bien vivre là-haut dans les arbres ?

Quand le rêve est fini, Lulu veut encore une aventure. Viens avec moi, allons voir le requin ! De quoi peut-il bien rêver ?

The shark plays tag with the fish. Finally he's got some friends! Nobody's afraid of his sharp teeth.

When the dream is over, Lulu wants to go on another adventure. Come along, let's visit the elephant! What could he be dreaming?

Le requin joue à chat avec les poissons. Enfin, il a des amis ! Personne n'a peur de ses dents pointues.

Quand le rêve est fini, Lulu veut encore une aventure. Venez avec moi, allons voir l'éléphant ! De quoi peut-il bien rêver ?

The elephant is as light as a feather and can fly! He's about to land on the celestial meadow.

When the dream is over, Lulu wants to go on another adventure. Come along, let's visit the little mouse! What could she be dreaming?

L'éléphant est léger comme une plume et il peut voler ! Dans un instant il
va se poser dans la prairie céleste.
Quand le rêve est fini, Lulu veut encore une aventure. Venez avec moi,
allons voir la petite souris. De quoi peut-elle bien rêver ?

The little mouse watches the fair. She likes the roller coaster best.
When the dream is over, Lulu wants to go on another adventure. Come
along, let's visit the dragon! What could she be dreaming?

La petite souris visite la fête foraine. Ce qui lui plaît le plus, ce sont les montagnes russes.

Quand le rêve est fini, Lulu veut encore une aventure. Venez avec moi, allons voir le dragon. De quoi peut-il bien rêver ?

The dragon is thirsty from spitting fire. She'd like to drink up the whole lemonade lake.

When the dream is over, Lulu wants to go on another adventure. Come along, let's visit the kangaroo! What could she be dreaming?

Le dragon a soif à force de cracher le feu. Il voudrait boire tout le lac de limonade !

Quand le rêve est fini, Lulu veut encore une aventure. Venez avec moi, allons voir le kangourou. De quoi peut-il bien rêver ?

The kangaroo jumps around the candy factory and fills her pouch. Even more of the blue sweets! And more lollipops! And chocolate!

When the dream is over, Lulu wants to go on another adventure. Come along, let's visit the knight! What could he be dreaming?

Le kangourou sautille dans la fabrique de bonbons et remplit sa poche.
Encore plus de ces bonbons bleus ! Et plus de sucettes ! Et du chocolat !
Quand le rêve est fini, Lulu veut encore une aventure. Venez avec moi,
allons voir le chevalier ! De quoi peut-il bien rêver ?

The knight is having a cake fight with his dream princess. Oops! The whipped cream cake has gone the wrong way!

When the dream is over, Lulu wants to go on another adventure. Come along, let's visit the monkey! What could he be dreaming?

Le chevalier a une bataille de gâteaux avec la princesse de ses rêves. Ouh-la-la, le gâteau à la crème a râté son but !
Quand le rêve est fini, Lulu veut encore une aventure. Venez avec moi, allons voir le singe ! De quoi peut-il bien rêver ?

Snow has finally fallen in Monkeyland. The whole barrel of monkeys is beside itself and getting up to monkey business.

When the dream is over, Lulu wants to go on another adventure. Come along, let's visit the pilot! In which dream could he have landed?

Il a enfin neigé au pays des singes. Toute leur bande est en folie, et fait des bêtises.

Quand le rêve est fini, Lulu veut encore une aventure. Venez avec moi, allons voir le pilote ! Sur quel rêve a-t-il pu se poser ?

The pilot flies on and on. To the ends of the earth, and even farther, right on up to the stars. No other pilot has ever managed that.

When the dream is over, everybody is very tired and doesn't feel like going on many adventures anymore. But they'd still like to visit the lion cub.

What could she be dreaming?

Le pilote vole et vole. Jusqu'au bout du monde, et encore au delà,
jusqu'aux étoiles. Jamais aucun pilote ne l'avait fait.

Quand le rêve est fini, ils sont déjà tous très fatigués, et n'ont plus trop
envie d'aventures. Mais quand même, ils veulent encore voir le bébé lion.

De quoi peut-il bien rêver ?

The lion cub is homesick and wants to go back to the warm, cozy bed.
And so do the others.

And thus begins ...

Le bébé lion a le mal du pays, et voudrait retourner dans son lit bien chaud
et douillet.
Et les autres aussi.

Et voilà que commence ...

... Lulu's
most beautiful dream.

... le plus beau rêve
de Lulu.

The authors

Cornelia Haas has been illustrating childrens' and adolescents' books since 2001. She was born near Augsburg, Germany, in 1972. She studied design at the Münster University of Applied Sciences and is currently a professor on the faculty of Münster University of Applied Sciences teaching illustration.

Foto: Ingrid Hagenreich

Ulrich Renz was born in Stuttgart, Germany, in 1960. After studying French literature in Paris he graduated from medical school in Lübeck and worked as head of a scientific publishing company. He is now a writer of non-fiction books as well as children's fiction books.

Do you like drawing?

Here are the pictures from the story to color in:

www.sefa-bilingual.com/coloring

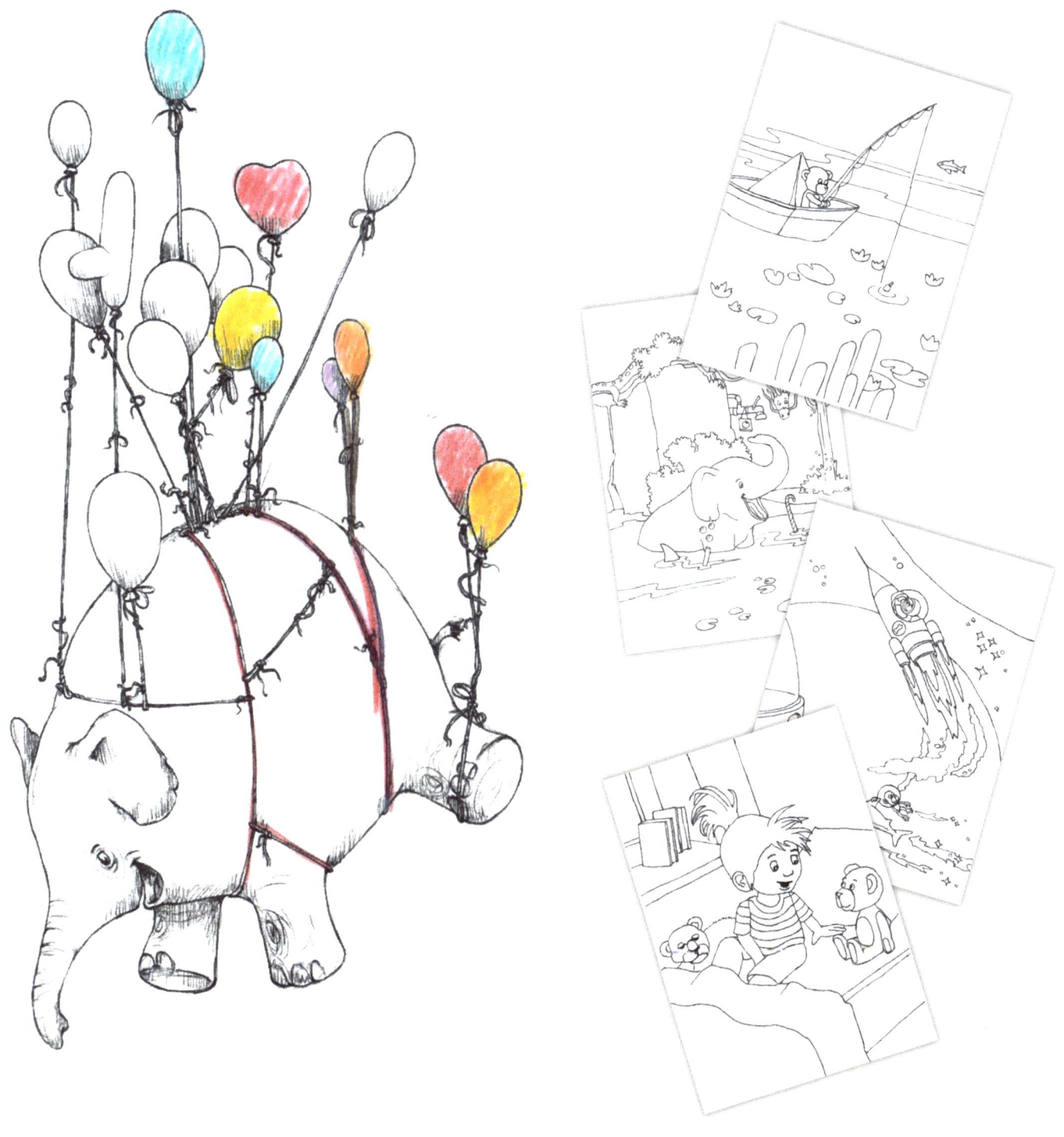

Sleep Tight, Little Wolf

For ages 2 and up

with online audio and video

Tim can't fall asleep. His little wolf is missing! Perhaps he forgot it outside?
Tim heads out all alone into the night – and unexpectedly encounters some friends...

Available in your languages?

► Check out with our „Language Wizard":

www.sefa-bilingual.com/languages

The Wild Swans

Based on a fairy tale by
Hans Christian Andersen

Recommended age: 4-5
and up

„The Wild Swans" by Hans Christian Andersen is, with good reason, one of the world's most popular fairy tales. In its timeless form it addresses the issues out of which human dramas are made: fear, bravery, love, betrayal, separation and reunion.

Available in your languages?

▶ Check out with our „Language Wizard":

www.sefa-bilingual.com/languages

© 2024 by Sefa Verlag Kirsten Bödeker, Lübeck, Germany

www.sefa-verlag.de

Special thanks for his IT support to our son, Paul Bödeker, Freiburg, Germany

ISBN: 9783739961637